CLEAR SPEECH

CLEAR
SPEECH

Practical Speech Correction
and Voice Improvement

Malcolm Morrison

Fourth edition

A &C Black · London

Fourth edition 2001
Third edition 1996
Second edition 1989
A & C Black (Publishers) Limited
37 Soho Square, London W1D 3QZ

ISBN 0–7136–5793–6

Originally published 1977 by Pitman Publishing Ltd

A CIP catalogue record for this book
is available from the British Library.

Printed in Great Britain by
Creative Print and Design (Wales), Ebbw Vale

Contents

Contents

Preface

Being mindful of the title and intent of this book, I have considerably revised and enhanced the chapter on Indistinct Speech. I have attempted to provide an improved explanation for this 'catch-all' term. In addition I have included exercises for the articulation of final consonants and some more exercises for the general agility of the organs of speech.

I am genuinely pleased that this book has had such an enduring impact and hope that this new edition with its improvements may prove to be equally helpful.

Using this Book

'I do not much dislike the matter, but the manner of his speech.'

Shakespeare, *Antony and Cleopatra*

How many people, in all walks of life, have had their career, even their personal relationships, marred by some little quirk of voice or speech that reduces their ability to communicate fully what they want to express? Yet it is surprising how easily and effectively such habits can be changed, given the necessary information.

There are thousands of people who need this kind of help: they may be dissatisfied with the quality of their voice, or they may feel that there are certain intrusive elements in their speech which are so distinctive as to draw attention to their mode of delivery rather than what they are trying to say. These are usually faults which can be corrected.

This is not to say that our voice or our manner of speech is not a highly personal expression of personality – it is. For that reason, this book makes no attempt to pass judgement on distinctions of dialect, nor to lay down some artificial definition of 'correct speech'. It leaves the reader free to make his or her individual decisions on the voice that he or she wants. Having made those decisions the techniques described here may be used to take the appropriate corrective action.

For example, the actor who has an unusual 'R' sound will very probably feel that that particular sound is not adequate to meet the needs of the variety of characters he or she must represent. So a change is made and the most common formation of the sound is acquired – he or she can also learn how to produce faulty formations if they best represent the character to be played. Likewise the public speaker who finds that the voice lacks strength or the authority to make the point may make a choice to

1

develop the required characteristics in his or her voice. In each of these cases, changes are being made in habits of voice or speech which may have been found perfectly satisfactory in ordinary conversation but are obviously unsatisfactory for specific situations.

The study of voice and speech can be complex. It is a subject beset by attitudes ranging from fear to bewilderment at its mystique. The aim of this book is to remove some of the fears and to unravel the mystique. Truly scientific study of the nature of voice and speech is a recent development, since only recently have we had the technology to provide sophisticated machinery which can measure with any exactitude the activities involved in producing speech. Over a very short period of time a large amount of knowledge has been accumulated on the formation of speech, and in these pages I have tried to present some of that knowledge, as simply and directly as possible. I have not attempted to produce an exhaustive textbook on phonetics, nor a study of those complex, often physiological problems of speech which are more appropriately dealt with by a qualified speech therapist. What I have covered are the problems I have most commonly met in a long period of professional voice teaching, with particular attention to those which respond to well-directed self-help.

In the sections that follow, therefore, you will first find the facts necessary to understand a particular problem – what is its cause, what is the correct formation – followed by tested, practical exercises to help bring about the correction required.

I have deliberately avoided the use of complex and unfamiliar technical terms, to keep the book readable and to enable even the inexperienced reader to follow its descriptions. This does not mean that the book renders a teacher superfluous. The teacher who reads this book will find a wealth of corrective exercises on which to draw, and be aware of the simplifications of terminology and analysis which have been made in order to stress the practical element in retraining the habit. Wherever possible, the non-expert should consult a teacher on the best use of this book and its exercise material. If, however, such help is not available, you should find that you can achieve a great deal for yourself by patient and careful application to the principles and exercises given here.

None of the faults analysed here is attributable to a physical or structural fault in the speech-mechanism – these must be the concern of trained professionals. We are concerned with the misunderstanding or mismanagement of an otherwise healthy instrument. The whole emphasis is on the readjustment of habits – a readjustment anyone can make through thorough, frequent, and informed practice of the material in these pages.

Speech as a Habit

Speech and the use of voice are habits which are built up and consolidated during the lifetime of an individual. From an early age one experiences the necessity and value of making verbal communication with another individual, and through a gradual process of imitation and selection the habit is formed. Just as a baby recognises that to point at something denotes interest in the object so he or she learns that to identify it verbally has the same effect. This involves the child in a serious study of recognition; first, of other people's capacity to verbalise, and then his or her own physical ability to form all the constituent sounds which accumulate into a message. In attempting to correspond with the verbal habits of the environment a child gradually begins to gain control over his or her voice and speech and to learn its value in bringing satisfaction to the appetites, whether physical or emotional.

Naturally, in developing the habit of voice and speech, only those features which ensure maximum effectiveness within the environment are acquired. For example where the intellectual demands are very small in the first years of life a child will require little subtlety of intonation or definition of sounds. As the demands for precision in thought and articulation are increased, so the habit of speech is modified and extended accordingly.

Since the habit of speech is acquired in specific response to the environment he or she will gradually build a habit to operate most effectively within that limited area. It may well be, and often is the case, that as a person grows older and his or her horizons, geographical, social and emotional, are extended he or she will find that certain early habit-patterns are of limited, or no, use.

The Nature and Analysis of Faults

Voice and speech problems divide themselves, simply, into three basic categories:

1. Those caused by some structural deficiency in the mechanism, for example cleft palate speech or hare lip.
2. Emotional and psychological problems.
3. Adequate mechanism but basic mismanagement of it.

It is not the scope of this book to deal with 1 and 2. These require the skills of Speech Therapists and suitably qualified medical practitioners.

In order to establish what a 'fault' in voice and speech is it is necessary to establish a Norm by which all other assumptions as to speech adequacy are relative.

These 'norms' are not universal and the discretion of the speaker or teacher has to be sensitively exercised to determine the relative acceptability of a problem. For instance the uvular R heard in French and German is not a usual element of English speech. As a result the use of such an R in English, although not inhibiting the understanding of the message conveyed by the speaker, would normally draw attention to itself and the *way* that the speaker is communicating. It is this element of *conspicuous* diction with which this book is concerned.

Normal, or rather adequate, speech is that form of verbal communication which may be anticipated in any given environment. It draws the least attention to the way in which a speaker communicates while expressing the message of the speaker with maximum control over his environment; and the realisation of all his objectives in terms of response from his audience.

It is easy to see the application of the foregoing statements in relation to speech, where the chances of a child speaking with a defective form of R sound are greater if the whole of his or her immediate family use the same kind of sound, but these principles apply equally to the production of voice. Examples are the family which permanently uses a high pitched voice, or the worker who develops an habitual loud volume as a result of competing with noisy machinery in his or her job.

Given that voice and speech are developed by habit it follows that, in order to effect a correction or modification, it is necessary to build up a new habit.

ANALYSIS OF FAULTS

In order to establish a clear understanding of the problems of a speaker it is necessary to approach the problem analytically. In general, given that the speaker possesses a healthy vocal instrument with no organic defect, the problems divide themselves into the following categories:

1. Problems of voice production. These are concerned with the basic sound which the speaker produces. Voice is the means by which we recognise the identity of a speaker.
2. Problems of articulation. These are the difficulties experienced in making specific speech sounds, individually and in combination, in any given language. Speech may be defined as the *pattern* of sound which we create by movements of the tongue, lips and soft palate.
3. Problems of delivery. Once the voice is adequately produced and the speech pattern is acceptable it is still possible that the delivery does not efficiently communicate the attitude of the speaker to the listener or to the subject matter. For example: the voice and speech may be technically exact, but the *rate* of delivery is too fast either for the listener to assimilate or for the speaker to express adequately the feeling implied.

The following list may provide a reasonable means of assessing the adequacy of voice and speech:

VOICE PRODUCTION

Quality	Pitch	Volume
Nasal	Generally too high	Generally too loud
Breathy	Generally too low	Generally too quiet
Hoarse	Erratic	Erratic
Thin and Strident	Monotonous	

ARTICULATION

Sounds omitted
Sounds added
Sounds substituted
Sounds defective

DELIVERY

Generally too slow
Generally too fast
Hesitant and confused

CORRECTION OF PROBLEMS

In order to establish a new habit of voice production or speech certain things are necessary:

1. *Recognition* of the problem.
2. *Information* concerning the fault and where it deviates from the desired model.
3. *Discrimination* either by hearing or feeling between the undesired habit and the correct one.
4. *Repetition* of exercises to establish the easy use of the new habit.
5. *Application* of achievement from exercises to everyday speech.

ATTITUDE TO CORRECTION

The effect of the attitude of the speaker, in achieving correction, cannot be under-estimated. Very often it is possible to achieve a state where the speaker is *capable* of making the new sound but is hesitant about its actual use in an everyday situation. It is this most important *bridging activity* between technical consideration and practical use which

7

causes the most problems and places an inhibiting respon-
sibility on the speaker. The logic of the situation is that if
one has recognised and attempted to correct some element
of speech it follows that it is more desirable not only to
speak that way but also to be *heard*. It is important to develop
the frame of mind where one concentrates on what a
listener would normally hear and therefore find acceptable,
rather than on what the speaker finds most usual.

It may be a truism, but it needs constantly bearing in
mind, that if one is going to *speak* differently then for a
time it will *feel and sound different*. But with constant,
conscious practice a new habit is formed and the acquired
habit will feel and sound perfectly normal to the speaker.

PRINCIPLES OF CORRECTION

There are various ways of approaching the problem of
correcting faults. It is difficult to say which of the methods
described below will be most successful. Generally any
result will depend upon the perception and application of
the speaker. The following are suggested as fairly broad
principles on which to base the work.

1. Where there is a problem on a specific sound in
speech it is utterly pointless merely to provide a piece of
practice material or a set of exercises in which repetition
of the sound is involved. This only serves to exaggerate
the problem and, with too much practice, to consolidate an
already undesirable speech habit. To provide a person
who has difficulties in making a satisfactory S sound with
jingles of the 'Sister Susie sewing socks for sailors' variety,
has absolutely no validity on its own. It is essential to
approach the problem methodically, with graduated exercises encouraging the development of the movements
required, culminating in the articulation of the sound itself.

2. It should be remembered that the appeal of a sound
to a speaker is not only auditory but is very often the
product of sensations in the mouth, nose and throat. While
the imitative kind of teaching *may* produce quick results it
may also serve only to confuse the speaker, who then has
to hear the difference in sounds, when the very reason why
he or she is producing inadequate voice and speech is
precisely because the hearing is limited in some way. This
is not to condemn entirely the use of imitation – but it is

only efficient if it works! Remember that listening and speaking may create different perceptions. For example, a speaker may feel that he or she is making extra effort whereas the listener will only perceive the additional effort as increased volume.

3. It may be that a visual approach will assist the speaker to make a correction. For example, a clear diagram of the position required for the tongue in the articulation of the sounds, or some kind of visual representation of the changes in pitch level in the voice, may well be helpful.

4. A clear account of the sensations involved in producing the sound, coupled with the speaker's ability to store and then reproduce that exact sensation each time, is also helpful.

5. More often than not a combination of the Imitative, Visual and Tactile approaches mentioned in 2, 3 and 4 will be needed.

6. It is impossible to bring about correction without *constant and frequent practice.* This cannot be emphasised too strongly. It is not sufficient to practice for a long time once a week. Regular daily practice is called for. Since the object of correction is to build a new habit, like other habits it must eventually become subconscious; and this can only be achieved if it is used often enough. Once the object of correction has been achieved then it requires frequent practice to maintain it.

7. Where more than one problem is involved – which are not inter-related – it is advisable to tackle each one separately and cumulatively. Rather than coping with several problems at once, try to determine a priority and deal with the most apparent and conspicuous difficulty first.

Relaxation

One of the greatest impediments to adequate voice production is the unnecessary use of muscles not directly required to assist in producing the sound. These muscles may be contracted and tensed to inhibit their effectiveness or may be deployed with an energy greater than is necessary to achieve the desired result.

As a preliminary to all work concerned with the voice, it is important to begin with simple limbering and relaxing exercises, in which the posture is adjusted and an appropriate elimination of unnecessary muscular effort is achieved.

There are various interpretations of the word 'relaxation' and it is important to make some definition of the term as it is applied to the production of voice – indeed of any physical activity. Relaxation, in this sense, is not that profound mental and physical state often associated with meditation, or near-sleep. It is simply the awareness and adjustment of the physical attitude of the body to ensure a correctly aligned posture with a minimal involvement of those parts of the anatomy not directly involved in the task.

For example, screwing up the hands into tight fists while speaking is a typical signal of unnecessary tension. Since the activity of all muscles is related, the tendency is for this tension to communicate itself to the arms, the shoulders and the neck. As a result the efficiency of breathing is impaired and the quality of the tone of the voice is liable to reflect this tension. Similarly to stick the chin forward, so that the underside of the jaw is showing, will produce a stretching and tension in the throat as well as a stiffness of the jaw, which interfere with the speaker's ability both to articulate individual sounds and to produce voice adequately.

This is not to suggest that the problem of tension is exclusively physical. The muscular signs may well be attributable to states of anxiety. By the very nature of the act of communicating verbally with other people, there is likely to be an inherent attitude of apprehension, even extending as far as deep fear. It is neither the province of this book, nor that of the teacher, to account for and deal with the complicated emotional states which are attendant on speech situations, beyond making some fundamental suggestions for coping with the *familiar* and *common* problems of anxiety which most people experience at some time or another.

The suggestions offered below are an attempt to help the speaker in rationalising his or her anxiety, followed by some suggestions to analyse what form the tension takes physically.

1. Always make sure that you understand and believe in what you are saying. This applies equally to conversation as to a prepared speech or lecture.

2. Remember that most listeners want to hear you speak personally, fluently and articulately. In fact they wish you to do well. It is amazing how much patience and goodwill a listener will exercise to hear someone else's ideas.

3. Speak simply, using only vocabulary and facts of which you are sure.

4. Wherever necessary and possible, prepare the material to be spoken.

SOME COMMON CAUSES OF TENSION

1. Fear of a hostile reception by the listener.
2. Doubts about the suitability of the subject matter.
3. Unfamiliar vocabulary and doubts about one's capability to express ideas adequately.
4. Fear of forgetting memorised speeches or quotations.
5. Uncertainty about one's appearance.
6. Feelings of inadequacy in the production of Voice and Speech.

In each case forethought, preparation and a positive attitude towards these fears will go some way towards alleviating them.

EXERCISES FOR PHYSICAL RELAXATION LEADING TO GOOD POSTURE

These are useful exercises to do at the beginning of voice practice. Remember that concentration is important – try not to let the attention wander. Note clearly and carefully the physical sensations of tension and release as they occur.

1.   Lie on the floor and stretch out, trying to make yourself as long as possible. Release this position until you are lying on your back, with the hands palms up at the side of you. Repeat this several times, feeling the contrast between the sense of tautness in the body and its easy slow release into a relaxed and comfortable position.

2.   Lying on the back, check each part of the body consciously, ensuring that there is no unnecessary effort anywhere. Try to be methodical, thinking of each part from the toes upwards, through the legs, the spine, the stomach, the torso, shoulders, arms, hands and finally the neck, head and face. If in doubt, deliberately tighten and tense that part of you and then release it.

3.   In a standing position, raise the arms above the head and stretch towards the ceiling. Hold this tight position for a moment or two and then allow the body to break at the waist, releasing the effort in the upper part of the body. The arms should flop down with the hands almost touching the floor and the head hanging freely between the arms. Gradually and very slowly bring yourself into a standing position, letting the head and shoulders hang down until you are almost erect. The sensation should be of the spine gradually uncurling from the base. The hands should hang easily and freely by your sides as you stand erect. This standing position should be achieved with the minimum of effort.

4.   To check for tension around the arms and shoulders, imagine you are pushing against a wall about one foot in front of you, at shoulder height. Gradually release the effort and allow the arms to fall heavily by your sides.

5.   Standing with the feet slightly apart, release the neck, so that your head falls heavily on to your chest. Raise it slowly until the head feels well balanced on the shoulders. Note the sensation as the head is raised with the minimum of effort. Repeat this exercise several times, imagining that the head gets heavier as it falls and lighter as it rises.

6.   Let the head fall to the back and then to the sides as described in exercise 5. In each case there should be no sensation of *placing* the head, but that it achieves the position on its own volition.

7. Stretch the arms out to the sides, extending them as far as possible. Hold this wide, stretched position for a moment or two and then release the arms, allowing them to fall heavily by your sides. Repeat this five times.

8. Raise the shoulders and try to touch the ears. Hold this position, note the tension, and then release them.

9. Push the shoulders forward, as if you were attempting to cause them to touch each other. Hold this position then let them spring back easily and effortlessly. Repeat this five times.

10. Lift the chest forward and up, until you feel a hollow in the centre of the back. Hold it there for a moment and then release the chest.

Posture

Frequently the quality of voice, or the ability to support the voice with adequate breathing, is impaired by unsuitable posture. The problem of unnecessary tension has been dealt with previously and its effect upon the general posture of the speaker is obvious.

In addition to faults in position being brought about by tension there are certain common faults which may occur due to any number of reasons, ranging from laziness to the effects of occupation on the habitual stance of an individual.

COMMON FAULTS

1. 'Slumping'. Where the rib cage is allowed to sink towards the pelvis and the spine is rounded. This can affect the efficiency of breathing.

2. Round shoulders. Where the back is rounded laterally and the shoulders stick forward.

3. Pushing the torso forward and upwards. This is the kind of stance popularly associated with the military and tends to encourage shallow breathing.

4. Shoulders raised towards the ears and pushed inwards towards the neck. This produces tension in the throat and affects the quality of voice.

5. Leaning back. Here the weight of the body is distributed over the heels with consequent tightening of abdominal and other muscles to compensate.

6. The head pushed forward in advance of the torso, with either a raising of the head to show the underside of the chin, or a sinking of the chin into the chest.

7. A pulling back of the head, with the chin back against the chest. The tensions produced in 6 and 7 again have an effect on the quality of the voice.

The correct posture on the right avoids the extremes of tension (left) and slackness or 'slumping' (centre)

RECOMMENDED STANDING POSITION

1. The feet may be slightly apart.
2. The general disposition of the weight should be slightly forwards.
3. The pelvis should be above the instep.
4. The torso should be directly above the pelvis; neither in front of nor behind it.
5. The abdominal muscles should feel braced without tension.
6. The torso should feel raised, but not stretched, away from the pelvis.
7. The shoulders should be directly above the pelvis and should be in line with the breast bone at the front.
8. The head should feel well balanced immediately above the shoulders. It should be neither in advance of them nor behind them.
9. The chin should be in a medial position, neither showing the underside of the jaw, nor pulled back allowing a 'double-chin' to form.

Where bad posture is habitual, the desired alignment of the body may feel very strange and tend to produce tension at first. It requires a good deal of conscious effort to achieve the position and then deliberate decision to retain it. All unnecessary tension employed to achieve that position should be eliminated.

EXERCISES TO IMPROVE GENERAL POSTURE

1.   Stand on the balls of the feet, letting the arms hang loosely by the sides. Gradually lower the heels, keeping the weight slightly forward. Try to retain the feeling of being tall and well balanced as the heels are lowered.

2.   Place a finger on top of the head and feel the spine lengthening to push against the finger. The sensation should be that one is growing taller without tension. The head should be well balanced on top of the shoulders, with no feeling of tension round the throat in an attempt to push against the finger. The whole effort of stretching should appear to come from the spine.

3.   Bend from the waist, allowing the arms to swing freely, almost touching the floor. Gradually come to a standing position imagining that each of the vertebrae in the spine is placed slowly and carefully, one on top of the other, in a vertical position, rather like making a tower with building blocks. The head should be placed on top of the last vertebra.

4.   Deliberately slump, allowing the ribs to sink towards the pelvis and the shoulders to round. Gradually feel yourself growing outwards and upwards as you come to a good standing position feeling taller and wider.

5.   Stand against a wall and feel the back of the head and the whole length of the spine contacting the wall. Gradually move away, trying to retain the sense of alignment in the spine and head.

PROBLEMS OF VOICE PRODUCTION

Faulty Breathing

An adequate breathing method is fundamental to all good voice production. A high percentage of vocal difficulty is attributable to breathing which is undeveloped or erratic in application to voice.

It should be remembered that breathing can provide the voice with either *Power* or *Duration*. These are alternatives – you should not speak at your very loudest while sustaining long phrases; it will surely lead to strain. An adequate breathing method will develop the capacity of the breath, with an increase in control over the muscles, in order that longer phrasing may be sustained. It will also develop the strength of the muscles to allow the speaker to produce voice at varying volumes with ease.

RECOMMENDED METHODS

The most popularly accepted form of breathing for speech is known as central, or more technically, intercostal-diaphragmatic breathing.

In this method the following sequence is employed:

1. The *lower* ribs swing outwards and upwards increasing the size of the chest (Thorax) laterally. Breath is drawn into the lungs.

2. The diaphragm (a double-dome shaped muscle separating the thorax from the abdomen) is caused to descend and the chest increases in capacity vertically, and further breath is drawn into the lungs.

17

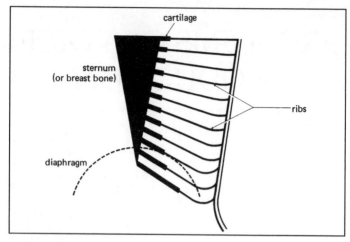

Schematic diagram of the rib cage, seen from the front, showing the position of the diaphragm

3.   The diaphragm is allowed to rise, while the ribs are retained in the raised position, and air is expelled.

4.   The ribs descend and further air is expelled.

It is important always to work in this sequence.

MAIN FAULTS

Clavicular breathing
Where very shallow breaths are taken into the upper part of the chest, providing very little capacity or control. It is often accompanied by a raising of the shoulders and a thrusting forward of the upper chest. It manifests itself in breathy tone and short phrasing from the speaker.

Abdominal breathing
This is more commonly found in men, where the ribs are hardly raised at all and the breath is taken immediately by the diaphragm. The whole of the lower abdomen, below the navel, is allowed to distend. Again the result is diminished capacity and little control over it.

Noisy breathing
Any adequate breathing method should provide for a noiseless inspiration of air. By constricting in the throat, through tension, or sucking the air in through partially closed teeth, a stricture is formed causing an audible friction as air is drawn into the body.

Lack of capacity
This manifests itself as an inability to sustain longer phrases. The speaker runs out of breath and the voice trails away. This may be due to insufficient control over the breathing muscles or a breathing method which does not successfully employ the use of both ribs and diaphragm. It could be that the speaker has an adequate supply but habitually taxes him- or herself to speak very long phrasing well beyond his or her natural capacity.

Lack of control
Breathy tone or erratic use of the volume of the voice may result from a lack of control over the breathing. In this case the most frequent cause is where the ribs are allowed to collapse at the same time as the diaphragm ascends. It may also be due to insufficient muscular control over the diaphragm and ribs causing them to collapse hastily and produce a 'heavy attack' on the first words in any phrase, with the rest of the phrase trailing away.

Lack of power
The speaker frequently feels that he is incapable of producing a loud enough volume. This is attributable to the strength of attack when expelling the air. The muscles may be weak and under-developed.

POPULAR MISCONCEPTIONS ABOUT BREATHING

1.   Air taken into the lungs does not push the ribs out. It is completely the reverse. The ribs are raised outwards and upwards and air rushes into the lungs to equalise the pressure.
2.   In taking a breath the lungs do not fill separately, one after the other. When the air is drawn in it fills the lungs simultaneously.

EXERCISES FOR BREATHING

When practising these exercises it is important to:

1.   Keep relaxed (see p. 11).
2.   Take in only the amount of air necessary to complete the exercise.

3. Work evenly and rhythmically.
4. Ensure that the shoulders and upper part of the chest are not raised.
5. Keep the lower abdominal muscles braced – without tension.

TO ESTABLISH THE MOVEMENT OF RIBS AND DIAPHRAGM

Method one

Lie on the floor and relax. Check that each part of the body, particularly the arms, shoulders and back, is not tense. Place one hand on the stomach, just below the end of the breast bone, and one hand on the lower ribs. Breathe in deeply and gently. During this ingoing breath the ribs will rise outwards and upwards, followed by the stomach rising. Do this very *slowly*. Breathe out and the stomach will descend followed by the ribs. Do this ten times slowly, feeling a definite separation between the movement of the stomach and the ribs. At first they may appear to work together, but with patience and concentration the separate movements can be developed.

It is important to remain calm and relaxed during this exercise. The exercise may be developed by gently sounding an OO sound as the air is expelled from the diaphragm and an AH sound when the ribs take over.

Method two

Standing up, breathe in and raise the arms outwards and upwards until they are stretched above the head. The movement of the arms will assist the movement of the ribs and help to sustain them in a raised position during the second part of the exercise. While the arms are raised pant in and out three times. The stomach will move in and out. The arms should then be lowered slowly as further breath is exhaled.

The exercise may be extended by slowing the inspiration and expiration of the breath while the arms are raised.

EXERCISES FOR CAPACITY AND CONTROL

The object of these exercises is to assist in increasing the amount of breath taken and the control to sustain longer phrasing in speech.

1. Using the ribs only. Breathe in for a slow count of three. Pause for a moment and then breathe out gently, with an open mouth, for a count of six. Raise the arms out to the sides, reaching shoulder height, on breathing in and lower them slowly while breathing out. This exercise should be done slowly and gently.

2. Do the same exercise but whisper the numbers on breathing out.

3. Extend the counting to nine, twelve, fifteen etc. Only add the additional numbers when the preceding stage can be achieved easily and comfortably.

4. Place the backs of the hands on the lower ribs and breathe in easily. Feel the ribs swing out. Gently blow the air out on an OO sound and feel the ribs swing in.

5. Repeat exercise 4 sustaining the OO sound for a count of ten.

6. Say the following, taking a slightly bigger breath on the ribs before each line. At the end there should be enough breath left to speak the sentence *twice* without taking a further breath:

I
I can
I can control
I can control my
I can control my breath
I can control my breath and
I can control my breath and sustain
I can control my breath and sustain my
I can control my breath and sustain my phrasing.

7. Swing the arms backwards, forwards, backwards while breathing in and then swing them forward to shoulder height breathing out on a long AH sound.

8. Breathe in, raising the arms to shoulder height at the side. Breathe out over a count of six, keeping the arms extended. Breathe in again, raising the arms above the head. Breathe out to a count of twelve, lowering the arms back to the side of the body.

9. Breathe in, raising the ribs, and whisper the following:

One and one are two
(*Breathe in again*)
Two and two are four
Four and four are eight

(*Breathe in again*)
Eight and eight are sixteen
Sixteen and sixteen are thirty two
(*Breathe in again*)
Thirty two and thirty two are sixty four
Sixty four and sixty four are one hundred and twenty
  eight.

10. Repeat number 9 with voice, beginning quietly and gradually increasing the volume as the exercise progresses.

11. Using the ribs and the diaphragm. Breathe in on the ribs and keep them expanded. Breathe in on the diaphragm and say 'January'. Follow this with further breaths on the diaphragm before saying each of the months of the year. The reserve of air in the ribs should be retained until the last diaphragmatic breath has been used on speaking 'December'. The exercise should then be completed by speaking all the months of the year using the air retained by the ribs.

12. Lie on the ground and place a book on the stomach, just below the sternum, or breast bone. Breathe in on the ribs and retain the breath. Breathe in and out, slowly, on the diaphragm and watch the book rising and falling.

13. Breathe in on the ribs, then in on the diaphragm. Using the breath from the diaphragm speak the following quietly. Renew the breath on the diaphragm at each /, but retain the air in the ribs as a reserve.

1/
12/
123/
1234/
12345/
1234/
123/
12/
1

After completing this exercise with diaphragmatic breath do *not* take a further breath after the count of 1 but speak the whole sequence through, smoothly and rhythmically, using the air retained by the ribs.

14. Speak the following quietly. Take a breath in on the ribs and then a breath in on the diaphragm. Renew the breath on the diaphragm at the end of each line, while retaining the raised rib position.

I
I saw
I saw three
I saw three snowmen
I saw three snowmen melting
I saw three snowmen melting away

On completion of the sentence do not take another breath on the diaphragm but use the reserve retained in the ribs to say 'away' as many times as you can comfortably manage.

15. Take a breath in on the ribs and the diaphragm and speak using the breath as shown:

From the diaphragm: A B C
From the ribs: D E F G H I J K L M
Breathe in again on the ribs and diaphragm.
From the diaphragm: N O P Q R S T U V W
From the ribs: X Y Z

16. Repeat exercise 15 but speak quite loudly on A B C and X Y Z. The longer phrases should be spoken quietly.

17. Take a breath in on the ribs and the diaphragm and then speak using the breath as shown:

From the diaphragm: A B C D E F G H I J K L M
From the ribs: N O P Q R S T U V W X Y Z

18. Speak the whole of the Alphabet twice – first using the air from the diaphragm followed by the air from the ribs.

19. Retain the reserve of air in the ribs and use only the breath from the diaphragm. Speak the following with a pause in place of the rhythmic count of four, do not take a breath. After the third phrase breathe and repeat the exercise:

One two three ——, one two three ——,
one two three ——.

20. Take a breath on the ribs and diaphragm. Count as high as you can, using the breath from the diaphragm. Then begin at 1 again and use the breath from the ribs to count as high as you can. Do not attempt more than you can *comfortably* achieve.

EXERCISES FOR POWER

The object of these exercises is to develop the strength of the muscles to develop volume of voice.

1. Place the hands on the lower ribs, press firmly and breathe in against the resistance of the hands to a count of three. Retaining the pressure of the hands breathe out to a slow count of nine.

2. Bend over with the body at right angles to the legs and the back as flat as possible. Breathe in and out gently and rhythmically on the lower ribs.

3. Sit cross legged on the floor, keep the back as straight as possible and breathe in and out gently to counts of six.

4. Breathe in on the ribs, breathe in on the diaphragm. Using the air from the diaphragm count up to ten slowly, gradually increasing the volume. Once the air from the diaphragm has been used then use the air from the ribs to count back, from 10 to 1, decreasing the volume. The exercise should end with a *whispered* count of 1.

5. Speak the following, taking a breath on the diaphragm at each /. The single count of one should be spoken loudly, employing all of the breath from the diaphragm. The longer phrases should be much quieter:

1/
1 2 3 4 5 6 7 8 9 10/
1/
1 2 3 4 5 6 7 8 9 10.

Repeat this several times.

6. Speak the following sentence, using breath from the diaphragm. Begin quietly and increase the volume towards the end of the sentence:

I can breathe quite freely and easily with good control, a large capacity and no apparent strain.

7. Place the palm of the hand approximately three inches from the mouth. Using breath from the diaphragm, speak the alphabet as the arm is gradually extended. Think of placing each letter in the palm of the hand.

8. Breathe in on the ribs and diaphragm. Let the breath go from the diaphragm on a loud, open, sigh on an OO sound. Follow this with an EE sound using the air from the ribs.

9. Repeat number 8 making the OO sound a quiet, gentle sound and the EE long and loud.

10. Take a breath on the ribs and diaphragm. Speak three loud, short OO sounds on the diaphragm, then let the air go from the ribs on a long, sustained and steady AH sound.

PRACTICE MATERIAL FOR BREATHING AND PHRASING

Read the following passages and mark in where you intend to breathe. Test your practical accomplishment in breathing by varying the length of phrase. Whisper them through first, then speak them with appropriate variations of pitch, pace and volume.

The wind stung them as they walked out of the hotel into the biting air. This was not a day for dallying and they set off, at a brisk pace, crunching their heels into the packed snow. The park was only a few hundred yards away, and as they passed through the huge iron gates they saw children of all sorts of shapes and sizes skating on the pond. With their scarves wrapped round them they looked like a vast gathering of mobile barrels with legs. There was a lot of noise and it cut through the wintry air with a keenness like the frost. James began to hurry, clinging to the hand of his little girl, and they whooped, whistled and laughed as they half ran, half slid towards the pond. At the edge the pair of them stopped with that instinctive caution reserved for first steps on to ice. Tentatively each put a foot forward and, in spite of the fact that there were hundreds on there skating and sliding already, they pressed on to the ice and established its security, before totally committing themselves to the frozen water. Once that ritual was over they parted hands and began to walk round the pond with heavy feet, almost as if they were trying to burn their footprints into it. Ice is not to be walked on, and before long, the two of them were in the middle sliding and slipping and, needless to say, falling on the vast wet, shiny January miracle.

The firm, slow beat of the drums, the creaking of the soaking planks of the ship and the steady rhythmic lap of the sea against the vessel, were the only things to be heard.

The Captain listened to the silence and clenched his telescope in his hands with a firmness that expressed his anxiety, but also the thrill that he felt as he saw the enemy sailing towards them. The gunners were all loyal, and well trained men. They had been with him before when, with his usual combination of impudence and cunning, he had scuttled other wayward galleons unfortunate enough to come within firing range. The gulls circled above, reminding him of the nearness of the enemy coastline and he knew he was taking a great risk. From somewhere below he heard the buzz of conversation as everything was set ready for his command to fire.

The pace of the game was fierce. Every spectator in the stands knew that these were the last few minutes and the players sensed it. They were all making a determined effort to win the day. The ball was passed down the right wing and O'Keefe took it deftly; he turned and began to run down towards the enemy's net. He neatly ducked and avoided the desperate tackle of his red-shirted opponent and started to veer in towards the centre. In front of him he saw a cluster of three men converging on him and he realised he would lose the ball. He clung to it for a fraction of a second and then kicked, lobbing the ball over the heads of the three. It bounced where he had hoped and Marsh ran in to settle it with his body. It bounced again and then Marsh smashed it with his right foot and the crowd roared and screamed and sang. Their hero had done it again and they yelled their passionate anthem to him with all the fervour of a nation victorious in war. The turf seemed greener, the weather seemed finer, the players were giants, not men!

'It's about time we were moving,' she said, leaning over and picking her shopping bag up from the floor. Some of the crumpled magazines fell from the bag, but she just cursed and gave the dog a push with her foot. Slowly she hauled herself to her feet, feeling a little better for the rest, and ambled off in the direction of the church. The sad, wiry animal yawned and heaved itself off in the direction of his slowly disappearing mistress. She turned and shouted, 'Rusty!' and the dog moved a little faster. The leaves were blowing down the gutters and the air was fresh. It stung her face. She gazed into the shops and caught the whiff of bread, freshly brought from the oven, in the baker's across the road. Her hands involuntarily rummaged in her pockets for money but there was nothing except a foreign coin which she'd found some three months before.

Inadequate Pitch Range in the Voice

Many speakers do not use anything like the potential range of voice which is available to them. The tendency is to restrict the voice to a few notes and, in consequence, the delivery is monotonous and boring.

MAIN FAULTS

Habitual high or low pitch
Here the speaker uses either the high or the low notes of the voice to the exclusion of the others. The use of an unchanging high pitch is also associated with tension, particularly when speaking in a demanding public situation.

Repeated tunes
Equally monotonous is the voice which repeats the same intonation pattern, usually with a fall at the end of the phrase. This has the effect of apparently concluding the statement.

Erratic pitch levels
Where the voice shoots up and down the pitch range, without any association with the thoughts expressed.

Baby tunes
Artificial use of pitch changes in speech, such as is associated with adults speaking to small children. Once again there is very little association between the subject matter and the range of voice employed.

CORRECTION

1.   It is important not to strain the voice to reach notes at the upper and lower extremes which are excessively difficult to make.

2.   An adequate and plentiful breath supply should be established.

3.   There should be a constant support for the voice from the breath during these exercises.

4.   While doing the exercises attention should be paid to the position and movement of the head, as there is a tendency to raise the head and thrust the chin forward when producing the high notes, and to pull the chin towards the chest for low notes.

5.   Perform the exercises at varying volumes.

EXERCISES

1.   Hum any tune, listening to the various notes produced.

2.   Continue humming the tune but stop at various points and count from 1 to 10 using the note on which you stop.

3.   Sing a tune on the following vowel sounds:

OO   OH   AW   AH   AY   EE

4.   Sing again and stop at various points to speak the six vowels on the one note.

5.   Using the vowels, speak one on a high pitch, one on a middle pitch and one on a low pitch; precede them with H:

HOO HOH HAW HAH HAY HEE
 HOO HOH HAW HAH HAY HEE
  HOO HOH HAW HAH HAY HEE

6.   Repeat exercise 5 but do it quickly so that it sounds like laughter.

7.   Repeat exercise 5 but begin on the low note and travel up to the high note:

  HOO HOH HAW HAH HAY HEE
 HOO HOH HAW HAH HAY HEE
HOO HOH HAW HAH HAY HEE

8. Speak each of the vowel sounds as if you were asking a question.

9. Repeat the vowels as if you were giving the answer to the question.

10. Combine the two. Ask the question on the vowel, then repeat it giving the answer. Do this very slowly, extending the range.

11. Speak the following taking a new, higher note for each word.

                                               higher.
                                   and
                            higher
                     climb
                 voice
             my
        make
     can
I

12. Speak the following taking a new, lower note for each word.

I
     can
         make
            my
                voice
                    go
                        lower
                       and
                           lower.

13. Sigh out on each of the vowels and count 1 to 5 when your voice settles on its lowest note.

14. Reverse this and run up the scale on the vowels, speaking from 1 to 5 on the highest note.

15. Repeat exercise 14 but stop at various places on the way up the scale and count from 1 to 5 on that note.

PRACTICE PIECES

The following passages have been written to provide opportunities for using the range of the voice extensively. For the purposes of exercise it is helpful to exaggerate slightly the range used. Remember, in addition, that variety of *volume* and *pace* help considerably to relieve the monotony of delivery.

(Contrast the general pitch level of the first part of the piece with the second part. Determine whether you think a high or low level is more appropriate.)

With a low moan the wind wound round the house, rattling the windows and shaking the massive oak door, until the iron bolts gave way with a resounding shudder. The sickly spectre, now quite clearly defined under the yellow moon, appeared from the forest and glided towards the house . . .

meanwhile . . .

in the drawing room Lady Penelope languidly sipped a long, cool glass of lemonade while listening to the dulcet tones of the flute played by her elegant companion.

(Notice that in addition to changes of pitch the variety of pace and volume will contribute to the effectiveness of the delivery of the piece.)

The football stadium was packed with thousands of eager fans, boisterously brandishing programmes, rattles and bells – all in support of their hero, who at this moment was careering down the wing, the ball apparently stuck to his toes; past one opponent, then another and another, until, with a mighty effort, he kicked the ball into the enemy's net . . . GOAL!

later . . .

back in the dressing room, with the deep satisfaction of conquerors, the men lay submerged in the warm relaxing water. The steam rose like mist around them as their aching and tense muscles thawed. Away from the noise of the crowd, with only the low murmurs of congratulations, many succumbed to sleep.

Graham was not in the least upset by the sight. He just stared at the wreckage and wondered what could have happened. People grow giant plants – yes. They water them, they watch them and plants grow. But this was, to say the least, a little out of the ordinary. The giant chrysanthemum which had been the subject of his every waking thought and the object of unprecedented devotion in his life (this year anyway) had withered. Withered was hardly the expression – it had grown smaller. What had been a huge golden sun in his life had now shrunk to the size of an unambitious dandelion. It wasn't dead, indeed it wasn't even dying, it was smaller. He rubbed his hand across his chest and bent towards it. He knew it was the same flower because this had rather unusual red tips to the petals. He peered at it for a while, half believing it wasn't true, and half expecting that at any moment it would rise again to its full round glorious self. But it didn't. It tiptoed on the top of the soil with all the perkiness of a five year old in a dancing display. Graham looked round, he wasn't quite sure why, maybe for help, maybe for consolation – none was there; only the irony of the sun beating down on the glass, golden rich and life-giving.

She sat swinging her legs on the park bench and munching her sandwiches. They were her favourites – cucumber. It was a perfect day and she gazed into the distance savouring the warmth of the sun and the sensation of the gentle breeze on her face. Her dog dashed between trees, panting madly and tearing off again in pursuit of a white butterfly. It seemed to hover in the air just long enough for the dog to catch up with it and then flickered away again, drawing the dog after it like a mad, infatuated slave. Jenny eased back on her seat and shifted her gaze over to a corner of the park where an old oak tree stood basking in the sunlight. As she stared aimlessly she thought she saw a long sallow face peer out from behind the trunk of the tree. An old face. She blinked and looked away. A moment or two later she looked again, just to satisfy herself that it was her imagination, but just at that moment the head bobbed out again. There was no question about it, there was someone behind the tree. But there was more than a face, there was a long thin neck and bony shoulders and the neck was attached to a body. After looking round once or twice the angular figure teetered out from behind the tree and stood for a while gazing into the sky. Jenny realised that the figure was an old lady wearing a long thin cloak of dark green down to her ankles. The old woman raised her arms towards the sky and with a voice like the sound of a brass gong she yelled 'Rain' into the air and then hitched up her cape, revealing what looked like blue and white football socks, and ran behind the tree again.

Faulty Tone

Tone is the term used to define the *quality* of voice employed by a speaker. It is difficult to predict what quality of voice is the most desirable, since the matter is highly subjective, and will, to a large extent, depend upon the individual speaker's requirements within any given environment. It is much more easy to describe certain qualities which are either harmful to the voice or generally considered unpleasing.

Pharyngeal or 'plummy' tone
The speaker generally places the voice in the lower register and accompanies this with an undue tension on the back of the tongue. The chin may be pulled in towards the chest with a minimal movement of the jaw.

Correction
1. Exercises to establish relaxed and controlled breathing.
2. Adjustment of the position of the head. Ensure that the chin is lifted and the head balanced on top of the shoulders – not in advance of them.
3. The opening of the jaw, particularly on the vowel sounds.
4. Exercises for the flexibility and relaxation of the back of the tongue.
5. Exercises for pitch range, particularly a fluent use of the higher and middle notes of the voice.
6. Exercises for the balanced use of the resonators. (See p. 36.)

Strident or 'hard' tone
The speaker tends to use the upper notes in the voice and to produce excess tension in the muscular walls of the throat. The chin is often thrust forwards and upwards. The sound appears high, hard and thin.

Correction

1. Exercises to establish relaxed controlled breathing.
2. Adjustment of the position of the head. The under-side of the chin should not be visible.
3. Vowel sounds 'yawned' out slowly and smoothly.
4. Exercises for pitch range, particularly a fluent use of the notes in the middle and lower registers.
5. Exercises for the balanced use of the resonators. (See p. 36.)

Nasal tone
There are two kinds of nasality:

1. Excessive nasal resonance. In which the soft palate, which normally forms a trap door between the throat and nose cavities, is wholly or partially lowered allowing the sound to pass down the nose continuously.
2. Insufficient nasal resonance. In which either the nasal passages are blocked, due to some physical cause, or the soft palate is held permanently in the raised position, preventing the passage of sound into the nose. This produces the 'cold in the nose' quality of voice.

The two kinds of nasality are referred to as Positive and Negative Nasality, respectively.

Correction

1. Exercises for the flexibility of the soft palate (see p. 73).
2. Exercises for the balanced use of the resonators (see p. 36).

Positive Nasality:
1. 'Yawning' sounds.
2. Retain the yawning sensation while speaking the sounds:

    OO   OH   AW   AH   AY   EE

3. Precede each of the vowels with M N or NG feeling the arching of the soft palate, into the yawning feeling, on the vowels.
4. Speak the following, ensuring that there is no change in the quality of the vowel:

BOO	MOO	DOO	NOO	GOO	NGOO
BOH	MOH	DOH	NOH	GOH	NGOH
BAW	MAW	DAW	NAW	GAW	NGAW
BAH	MAH	DAH	NAH	GAH	NGAH
BAY	MAY	DAY	NAY	GAY	NGAY
BEE	MEE	DEE	NEE	GEE	NGEE

Negative Nasality:

1. Check that there is no structural reason why sound may not pass down the nose. This can be done simply by holding a finger against each nostril in turn and blowing down the other.

2. Hold the nose gently, but firmly, between the fingers and hum. Feel the sound passing positively down the partially constricted nasal passages.

3. Sing a simple tune on MOO, still slightly constricting the nose with the fingers, and sustain the sensation of the sound passing down the nasal passages.

4. Speak the following, ensuring that there is a clear distinction between the pairs of words. They can only be defined by making a clear M and N sound as opposed to B and D

Me	Bee	Note	Dote
Moat	Boat	Not	Dot
Melt	Belt	Gnome	Dome
Meant	Bent	Nine	Dine

It helps to make a long, sustained M and N, to begin with. As ability increases the length of the M and N sounds can be gradually decreased.

Husky tone

It should be noted that this may well be a strong indication of a structural defect in the vocal mechanism. Initially it is important to rest the voice, for approximately three days. After this period of silence, when the voice is not used *at all*, if the voice is still very husky, medical advice should be taken. Huskiness is often the precursor of loss of voice and the *only* valid treatment is rest. If the huskiness is spasmodic it may be due to strain resulting from excessive tension in the muscles of the throat and shallow breathing.

Correction

1.   Exercises to establish relaxed, deep breathing (see p. 21).

2.   Gently make the following sounds on a whisper, sustaining each one. Feel the arching of the back of the throat, as if yawning:

OO   OH   AW   AH   AY   EE

3.   Intone the vowels, quietly.

4.   At all times avoid shouting. Develop the habit of speaking very quietly, until the basic quality of the voice is established.

5.   General exercises for the balanced use of the resonators.

Breathy tone

This is due to an incomplete closure of the vocal cords during the formation of the sound, allowing air to escape between the cords. It is often the result of an inadequate breathing method where, for example, the ribs collapse very quickly and more breath is released than is needed to produce sound. It is a voice quality most often associated with Clavicular Breathing.

Correction

1.   A good deal of time should be spent on establishing an adequate breathing method.

2.   For short periods during exercise, the voice should be used quite loudly. Practice can include reading a passage from a newspaper or book, gradually decreasing the volume. As soon as the breathy quality is heard the volume should be slightly increased and then diminished again as the sound is established. It is important to avoid tension in the throat while practising.

3.   Exercises for the balanced use of the resonators.

BALANCED USE OF THE RESONATORS

The resonators are the hollow cavities above the voice box (larynx), in which the basic note produced by the vocal cords is amplified. The general aim is to achieve the effective use of each cavity (pharynx, mouth and nose) without a predominance of tone from any one resonator. When doing the following exercises it is essential to establish:

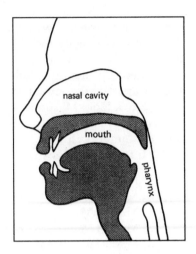

Positions of the resonators

1. Good posture, where the head is held easily on top of the shoulders. The chin should be neither thrust forward nor pulled back towards the chest.

2. Good support for the voice from the use of adequate breath.

3. Regular practice of breathing and the following exercises.

EXERCISES

1. Hum any tune gently. Beware of pushing the voice from the throat. Feel for a tickling sensation around the lips. Avoid any sense of strain. Take fairly short phrases, which can be well supported by the breathing. The lips should be *lightly* held together, with the teeth very slightly apart.

2. Whisper the following vowels. Sustain each sound for a count of six and ensure that there is no rasping in the throat.

OO   OH   AW   AH   AY   EE

3. Repeat 2 but arch the palate at the back of the mouth, as if yawning.

4. Repeat the six sounds imagining each sound is a bubble in the mouth. Blow them out gently on a whisper. Any harsh attack by the voice will burst the bubble.

5. Count up to ten trying to get an echo from the room. Do not 'push' the sound, think of 'drawing' it from the walls and ceiling.

6. Stand close to a wall and hum on a steady sustained 'M' sound. Gradually move away from the wall thinking of leaving the voice there.

7. Keeping the lips lightly together, but the teeth slightly apart, make a number of 'M' sounds, as if laughing.

8. Say a long 'M' sound as if in response to something pleasant. Repeat this five times, allowing the voice to become louder each time.

9. Intone the following:

M.M.M.M.M.	MOO
M.M.M.M.M.	MOH
M.M.M.M.M.	MAW
M.M.M.M.M.	MAH
M.M.M.M.M.	MAY
M.M.M.M.M.	MEE

10. Intone the following on one continuous note:

EE ... OO ... M.M.M.

11. Repeat 10 at various pitches.

12. Intone MOO MOH MAW MAH MAY MEE with the hands cupped round the mouth for M and opening them for the vowel. There should be a sensation that the voice is *released*.

13. Cup the hands over the ears and say 'Good morning'. There should be a sensation that the voice is outside of the head. Do this at various pitches.

14. Repeat the following sounds several times, keeping the voice on the mask of the face:

N   M   NG

15. Place each of the sounds in 14 before these vowels:

OO   OH   AW   AH   AY   EE

16. Whisper the following sentences:

Many moaning men making music to the moon.
Many merry milkmaids.
No never alone.
Nineteen noisy gnomes.
Singing swinging songs.

17. Intone the sentences in 16, on one note.
18. Speak the sentences, with a variation in pitch.

19.   To encourage the movement of the soft palate, keep the mouth open and breathe in through the nose and out through the mouth several times.

20.   Count slowly up to ten, first on a whisper, checking that there is no tension in the throat and that the whisper is full, clear and round. Then intone it slowly on one note, like a bell tolling. Finally speak it clearly, imagining the voice on the mask of the face.

Routines for the Establishment of Forward Placing of the Voice

The following routines are provided to give progressive, general exercise in placing the voice. They could form the nucleus of daily practice, with a change of routine each day to add variety to the daily discipline.

ROUTINE 1

1. Whisper the following vowels:

    OO   OH   AW   AH   AY   EE

Sustain each of them for a count of six. Ensure that the throat feels free and that there is no 'rasping' in the throat. Repeat this five times.

2. Whisper each sound, imagining that you are inflating a balloon gently and smoothly. The balloon should not inflate in jerks, but expand continuously and smoothly.

3. Breathe out on an OO sound, experiencing and noting the ease with which this is done. Feel for the air passing over the lips and then speak, quietly, 'one, two, three' keeping the sensation of the voice on the lips. Repeat this using the other vowels.

4. Intone, on one note, three short OO sounds followed by an 'M' sound, which should be sustained for a count of six:

    OO   OO   OO   MMMMMMMMMMMM
    OO   OO   OO   MMMMMMMMMMMM.

Repeat this exercise using each of the other vowel sounds to precede the 'M' sounds. Try to think of opening the throat on the vowel sounds and catching the voice on the mask of the face with the humming sound.

5.   Hum three short M sounds followed by one long 'M' sound:

M   M   M   MMMMMMMMMMM.

Repeat this five times.

Feel that the voice is placed on the mask of the face and that vibrations can be felt around the lips and nose.

6.   Whisper, intone on one note and then speak the following sentences:

Mining minerals in mountains.
Many military matters mustn't mount.
Nanny nodded nonchalantly.
Anonymous nonentities.
No names may be mentioned.

ROUTINE 2

1.   Repeat the following, feeling the release of the voice into the mouth after K and then the vibration in the nose on the NG N and M sounds. Make this sequence of sounds quiet and continuous, feeling for the sensation of the voice moving forwards:

K...AH...NG   K...AH...NG   K...AH...NG
K...AH...N   K...AH...N   K...AH...N
K...AH...M   K...AH...M   K...AH...M

2.   On the following sequence whisper the H sound, feeling a yawning sensation in the mouth, and then voice the vowel sounds retaining the yawning sensation. The vowels should sound full and rich:

HHH . . . OO	HHH . . . OO	HHH . . . OO
HHH . . . OH	HHH . . . OH	HHH . . . OH
HHH . . . AW	HHH . . . AW	HHH . . . AW
HHH . . . AH	HHH . . . AH	HHH . . . AH
HHH . . . AY	HHH . . . AY	HHH . . . AY
HHH . . . EE	HHH . . . EE	HHH . . . EE

3.   Feel the voice 'popping' off the lips after the B sound:

BAH	BAH	BAH	BOO
BAH	BAH	BAH	BOH
BAH	BAH	BAH	BAW
BAH	BAH	BAH	BAY
BAH	BAH	BAH	BEE

4.   Feel the voice vibrating gently on the lips throughout this exercise:

MAH	MAH	MAH	MOO
MAH	MAH	MAH	MOH
MAH	MAH	MAH	MAW
MAH	MAH	MAH	MAY
MAH	MAH	MAH	MEE

5.   Whisper the following piece, then intone it on one note, concentrating on placing the voice forward in the mask of the face. Finally speak it:

Above, the Gothic arches met, and in the dark blue spaces between them faint gold stars were twinkling. The deep blue of the painted spaces seemed limitless in the dim light of the lamp. Now and then the squeak of a foraging mouse sounded among the canvases. Old Grimes had been breathing heavily; now he raised himself on the bed, and lifting his arms, cried out, 'My masterpiece! Give me brushes, someone!'

Try to give full value to all the M N and NG sounds.

ROUTINE 3

1.   Feel a strong, vigorous movement of the soft palate during the repetition of the following sounds. Intone them on one note:

NG ... AH   NG ... AH   NG ... AH

2.   Repeat the following, listening for a continuous humming sound on the three M sounds, but very little passing down the nose on the vowel:

OO ... MMM	OH ... MMM	AW ... MMM
AH ... MMM	AY ... MMM	EE ... MMM

3.   Replace the M sound in exercise 2 with N and repeat.
4.   Hum on an M sound before intoning each of these words. Again do it quietly, feeling the vibrations on the lips and the release of the voice on the vowels:

M ... WE	M ... WILL	M ... WORRY
M ... WHILE	M ... WE	M ... WAIT

5.   Repeat the following sounds, first whispered, then intoned and finally, spoken. In each case sustain the M and

N sounds. Listen for the resonance as a continuous humming sound as you say the complete word:

many   many   many   many   many   many   many
minimal   minimal   minimal   minimal   minimal
ammonia   ammonia   ammonia   ammonia   ammonia
nominate   nominate   nominate   nominate   nominate

6. Following the usual sequence whisper, intone and then speak this passage from *St. Cecilia's Day* by Dryden. Sustain the resonance of the voice when speaking:

> From Harmony, from Heavenly Harmony,
>> This universal frame began:
>> From Harmony to Harmony
> Through all the compass of the notes it ran,
> The diapason closing full in many.

Give full value to the M and N sounds.

ROUTINE 4

1. Whisper, then intone the following:

OON NOO / OHN NOH / AWN NAW /
AHN NAH / AYN NAY / EEN NEE /
OOM MOO / OHM MOH / AWM MAW /
AHM MAH / AYM MAY / EEM MEE /
OONG NGOO / OHNG NGOH / AWNG NGAW /
AHNG NGAH / AYNG NGAY / EENG NGEE /

2. Whisper the first OO sound in the following sequence. Feel that there is no strain or unnecessary tension in the throat. Voice the M sound, feeling the voice forward on the mask of the face. Finally sustain the following vowel on one note:

OO . . . . M . . . . OO
         (Whisper)   (Intone)
OO . . . . M . . . . OH
OO . . . . M . . . . AW
OO . . . . M . . . . AH
OO . . . . M . . . . AY
OO . . . . M . . . . EE

3. Sustain the following sequence of sounds on an intoned note. Feel the voice moving forward towards the mask of the face as you do it:

```
EE . . . . . . . . . . OO . . . . . . . . . . M . . . . . . . . . . OO
EE . . . . . . . . . . OO . . . . . . . . . . M . . . . . . . . . . OH
EE . . . . . . . . . . OO . . . . . . . . . . M . . . . . . . . . . AW
EE . . . . . . . . . . OO . . . . . . . . . . M . . . . . . . . . . AH
EE . . . . . . . . . . OO . . . . . . . . . . M . . . . . . . . . . AY
EE . . . . . . . . . . OO . . . . . . . . . . M . . . . . . . . . . EE
```

4.   Whisper the following sentences with full, round vowels, then intone them on one note and, finally, speak them:

Who are you
We are three
All hard law
Slow past go
May's last day

5.   Conclude this routine by intoning, very gently:

HOOMING	HOHMING	HAWMING
HAHMING	HAYMING	HEEMING
MOONOOMOO	MOHNOHMOH	MAWNAWMAW
MAHNAHMAH	MAYNAYMAY	MEENEEMEE

SPEECH FAULTS

Introductory

The following section is concerned with the ability to make specific individual sounds of English.

Once the voice is produced it is shaped into particular types of sound by the use of the lips, tongue, hard palate, soft palate and the teeth.

The organs of speech:
1   Lips
2   Teeth
3   Alveolar ridge
4   Hard palate
5   Soft palate
6   Uvula
7   Tip and blade of tongue
8   Front of tongue
9   Centre of tongue
10 Back of tongue

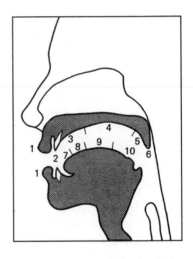

The diagram shows a sectional view of the organs of speech. Note that the tongue, for the purposes of describing the formation of sounds, is divided into various parts. There is no commonly used sound which employs the use of the uvula; although sounds made with the back of the tongue in conjunction with the uvula are frequent in other European languages, such as French and German.

In addition to the specific exercises given for correction of a sound, general articulation exercises should also be practised in order to develop dexterity and control of the lips, tongue and soft palate.

The English R Sound

The most common 'R' sound in English speech is known as a post-alveolar frictionless continuant.

To form this sound
The soft palate is raised to prevent the passage of air through the nose. The tongue tip is curled back behind the gum ridge, while the side rims of the tongue contact the upper side teeth. *It is important that the tongue does not make contact with the roof of the mouth.* The teeth are held slightly apart. The lips are usually held in a neutral position, although they may round if the sound is followed by a vowel with lip rounding such as OO or AW.

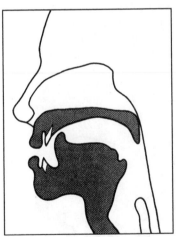

Formation of the R sound

Occurrence of R in English
R is usually pronounced before or between vowels. In common English speech it is never said when it precedes a consonant. This rule applies to the speaking of a word: not to its spelling. For example in the spelling of the word 'deferred' the R appears before a vowel; but when we speak it it would have to be said before a consonant, therefore,

in accordance with the rule, the R sound is NOT pronounced in the word 'deferred'.

The forgoing rule is not true of American English, where the **R** sound **IS** said before consonants and at the ends of words. Usually the **R** which is heard at the end of a word like 'other', is not a separate sound from the vowel but is actually a curling back of the tip of the tongue as the vowel is said. This curling back of the tongue during the formation of a vowel is known, technically, as retroflexion.

When, in connected speech, the R sound is followed by a vowel beginning a succeeding word, it is customary to pronounce the R and this is known as 'linking R'. For example, in the sentence 'There is a book', the R is followed immediately by the 'I' of is and the R sound would usually be spoken.

MAIN FAULTS

Uvular R

Occasionally a variety of R is heard where the uvula is allowed to vibrate against the back of the tongue, or air is forced between the uvula and the back of the tongue with audible friction. This is frequently heard from French and German speakers of English. It is a feature of certain varieties of North Eastern Dialect.

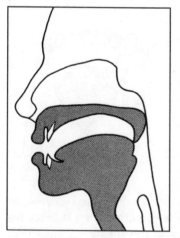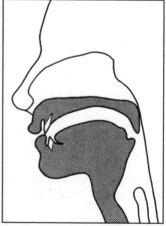

The position of the organs of speech in uvular R (left) and labio-dental R (right) is in strong contrast to the correct position shown previously

W substitute
This is a direct substitute of a perfectly normal W sound
in place of R.

R made with the teeth and lower lip
Technically, this is known as a labio-dental R. It is formed
by keeping the tongue relaxed in the mouth and bringing
the upper front teeth in contact with the back of the lower
lip.

CORRECTION

To obtain the correct R it is important to appreciate the
following points:

1. It is an *entirely different* sound from any of those
listed as faulty. It is impossible to modify any one of these
sounds to produce the correct sound.
2. The teeth must be slightly apart.
3. The *back* of the tongue must not rise – and certainly
must not contact the uvula or soft palate.
4. The tip of the tongue must curl back in the mouth.
5. The tongue tip should contact neither the gum ridge
nor the roof of the mouth.
6. This sound is 'vowel-like' inasmuch as there is no
audible friction or explosion, as with many consonant
sounds.

EXERCISES

1. For the mobility and flexibility of the tongue: Repeat
several L sounds in a variety of rhythms:

   11L   11L   11L   11L

vary the rhythm and gradually increase the speed and
dexterity with which it is done, without losing clarity of
each individual sound.
2. Repeat the following:

   SH   LLL/   SH   LLL/   SH   LLL/

note the curling back of the tongue to form SH.

3. T   SH   SH   SH/   T   SH   SH   SH/
   T   SH   SH   SH/

4. SH   SH   SH   T   T   T/   SH   SH   SH   T   T   T/
   SH   SH   SH   T   T   T/

FORMING R – METHOD 1

1. Say a long, sustained SH sound followed by the vowel ER. *Keep the tongue in the position for SH as you try to say ER.* The sound produced should approximate to a R sound.

2. Repeat the exercise above, but follow the ER sound with the following vowels. Make sure that after the ER the tongue falls from behind the gum ridge to behind the lower teeth:

SH ER OO / SH ER AW / SH ER AH /
SH ER AY / SH ER EE.

It is important to keep the tongue curled back while speaking the ER sound in this exercise.

3. Using a mirror, say ER and continue to make the sound as the tongue is curled back behind the gum ridge. The tongue should be raised to show its underside in the mirror.

4. Repeat exercise 3, but make a long, continuous ER sound and raise and *lower* the tongue to behind the lower teeth. The movement of the tongue should be done strongly. At no time should the tongue contact either the gum ridge or the hard palate. This exercise should be repeated until a strong R is heard when the tongue is lowered.

5. Say a long ER sound, at the same time curl the tongue behind the gum ridge. Lower the tongue sustaining the vowel ER and then form the following vowels when the tip of the tongue is behind the lower teeth:

ER R OO / ER R OH / ER R AW /
ER R AH / ER R AY / ER R EE

6. Once the R sound has been achieved in association with SH and ER, repeat the following words, three times each:

SHRINK SHROUD SHREW SHRILL SHRED.

As the R is formed feel the tongue curl just a little further back in the mouth and move away from the gum ridge.

7. Having established the R sound in conjunction with SH, speak the following words, forming SH but *making no sound*. Only make the word audible when the tongue is drawn back for the R sound:

(SH)   RED   (SH)   RULE   (SH)   RISE
(SH)   RING   (SH)   RATE

8.   When the R has been established in this way, use the list of words at the end of this section for practice.

Remember the CURLING back of the tongue; do it slowly and gradually speed up.

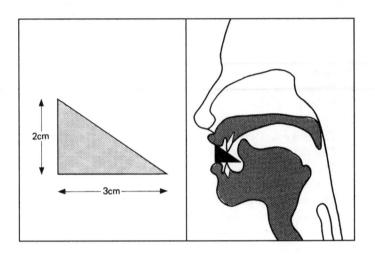

FORMING R – METHOD 2

1.   Use the exercises on page 73 for mobility and flexibility of the tongue.

2.   Cut a piece of fairly thick card to the dimensions shown and hold it in the position illustrated in the diagram, between the front upper and lower teeth.

Say the following vowel sounds, making sure that the tongue is curled back and does not, at any time, fall to touch the point of the card. A sound approximating to R should be heard:

OO   OH   AW   AH   AY   EE

3.   Repeat exercise 2 but speak the vowel again, after the R is heard. At the same time remove the card and allow the tongue tip to fall behind the lower teeth.

OO   R   OO   /   AW   R   AW   /   AH   R   AH   /
ER   R   ER   /   EE   R   EE

4.   Repeat exercise 3 without the assistance of the card.

5.   Continue practice with the words that follow.

Remember to keep the teeth apart and the tongue curled, without contacting the roof of the mouth, on the R sound.

Words to practise R

red   rich   round   rule   rope   read   wrong   wreck   wretch

arrange   derive   borrow   worry   thorough   serious   sorrow   lorry

dressed   prim   break   train   shrink   throb   fry   great   spread   crime

Sentences to practise R

Bring three lorries round to the front.

Raise the retail price.

The rusty rod was wrapped in a rotting rag.

The story concerned a marriage arrangement in Norwich.

The river runs under the railway bridge.

Carry the dress round to the rest room.

The grain was really very brown.

The mourners preceded the funeral carriage.

The rope broke sending them sprawling into the drink.

It's really rather a curious reason.

The S Sound

Description
This sound is known as an Alveolar Fricative. Z as in zoo is formed in the same way but is *voiced*.

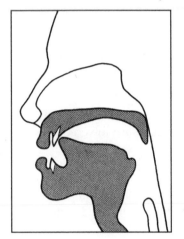 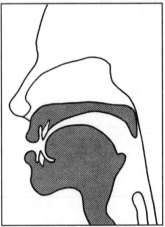

Left, the normal formation of S. Right, the alternative described below

To form this sound
1.   The soft palate is raised to prevent the passage of air through the nose. The tip and the blade of the tongue are raised to make very light contact with the alveolar ridge. The sides of the tongue are held against the upper side teeth. The air is forced along a narrow channel down the centre of the tongue and causes friction, which is audible, between the tongue and the alveolar ridge. The teeth are held very slightly apart and passage of the air over the cutting edge of the upper front teeth is an important feature of the sound.

2.   Although the method described in 1 is the most common, many speakers form a perfectly acceptable variety of S by placing the tip of the tongue behind the lower teeth

and humping the tongue to bring the blade in light contact with the alveolar ridge.

MAIN FAULTS

Labio-dental S
Some speakers make an additional contact with the upper front teeth and the lower lip.

TH substitution
This is where there is direct substitution of a perfectly normal TH sound in place of S.

Dental S
Instead of bringing the tip of the tongue in light contact with the alveolar ridge, the tip of the tongue is placed on the hinder part of the upper front teeth.

Lateral S
The tip of the tongue makes *firm* contact with the alveolar ridge, while the sides of the tongue are lowered allowing the air to escape laterally.

'Whistly' S
This is caused by excessive tension on the tongue, with a consequent increase in the tightness of the channel down which the air is forced.

Other problems
If there is any serious irregularity in the teeth, particularly the upper front ones, it is likely that the S sound will be faulty. For example, dentures may cause the sound to be slightly muffled since there is an increased bulk at the alveolar ridge and the cutting edge of the teeth may not be sharp enough.

Gaps in the front teeth also tend to influence the quality of S produced.

CORRECTION

1.   S is a difficult sound to make and requires *fine* adjustments in the tongue. The tip of the tongue should only make *very light* contact with the alveolar ridge. Study carefully the description (at the beginning of this section) of

how this sound is formed. It is most important to identify *where* the sound is formed.

2.   If particular difficulty is experienced in making S, both methods of formation should be tried to see which one produces the more satisfactory result.

3.   It is important that the speaker should keep relaxed during the exercises, since any undue anxieties may express themselves in tension in the tongue.

4.   Care should be taken not to build up too much air pressure in forming this sound.

5.   The sound should not be unduly sustained – the aim should be to produce a short, sharp sound.

FORMING S – METHOD 1

1.   Repeat several T sounds in the following rhythmic pattern:

ttT   ttT   ttT   ttT   ttT

2.   Repeat exercise 1 but allow the tongue to release *slowly* on the stressed sound in each group. Maintain the breath pressure and a sound similar to S will result.

3.   Speak the following, beginning with T and releasing slowly into the S and then continuing, without pause, on to the vowel:

TSOO   TSOH   TSAW   TSAH   TSAY   TSEE

4.   Repeat exercise 3. Begin with the tongue in position for T and release it slightly before applying breath.

5.   If the S is emerging, but sounds rather muffled, spread the lips slightly and concentrate on directing the air across the cutting edge of the upper front teeth, with a short, sharp sound. It sometimes helps to think of the air being directed towards the canine teeth.

6.   Once the sound is fairly secure, practise the following slowly, noting the lifting and dropping of the tongue to form S. Remember only light application of the tongue to the gum ridge is needed:

OO   S   OO   /   OH   S   OH   /   AW   S   AW   /
AH   S   AH   /   AY   S   AY   /   EE   S   EE   /

7.   Practise the following noting the difference in tension between the tongue position for S compared with T:

OOST / OHST / AWST /
AHST / AYST / EEST /

8. This drill should be continued daily until the sound can be formed with ease and then practice of the words and sentences which follow should be undertaken.

FORMING S – METHOD 2

1. Repeat several TH sounds, as in *th*ick, in the following rhythmic pattern:

th th TH / th th TH / th th TH /

2. Repeat exercise 1 but sustain the last TH sound in each group. As the TH sound continues, pull the tongue back in the mouth, slowly, allowing the tip to brush against the back of the upper teeth and the gum ridge. As it passes over the ridge a sound similar to S will be heard.

3. Repeat exercise 2 but increase the breath pressure when the tongue reaches the gum ridge.

4. Say a long TH sound and draw the tongue straight back from the upper teeth to the gum ridge. Practise this movement in various rhythmic patterns.

5. Practise the following quickly, making each sound very short:

TH S / TH S / TH S / TH S /

6. Contrast the tongue position for the following:

OO TH OO — OO S OO /
OH TH OH — OH S OH /
AW TH AW — AW S AW /
AH TH AH — AH S AH /
AY TH AY — AY S AY /
EE TH EE — EE S EE /

7. Feel the tongue moving alternately from teeth to gum ridge as you speak the following:

TH OO S / TH OH S / TH AW S /
TH AH S / TH AY S / TH EE S /

8. If the sound produced for S seems tight and whistly, think of spreading the sound along the cutting edge of the upper front teeth. It sometimes helps to think of directing the air to the canine teeth.

FORMING S – METHOD 3

This method should be adopted if it is impossible to gain a satisfactory result from either Methods 1 or 2.

1.   Make several of the sounds usually described in novels as 'tut tut'. It is a clicking sound made with the blade of the tongue against the alveolar ridge.

2.   Note the position of the tongue in exercise 1, but try to place the tip of the tongue behind the lower teeth and repeat the sound.

3.   Again, note the position of the tongue in exercise 2, but instead of sucking air in the click, blow the air out strongly over the held tongue position. A sound similar to S should result.

4.   Alternate this S sound with a sound similar to T, and with the tip of the tongue held behind the lower teeth and the blade of the tongue applied to the gum ridge.

T   S   /   T   S   /   T   S   /   T   S   /

The sound may be a little muffled and every attempt should be made to keep the teeth very slightly apart and the lips away from the teeth – like a smile.

5.   Repeat the T S combination with the tongue tip held behind the lower teeth but continue the sound into a vowel:

T   S   OO   /   T   S   OH   /   T   S   AW   /
T   S   AH   /   T   S   AY   /   T   S   EE   /

6.   Place the tongue in position for this S sound and, making a very short S, continue into the vowel:

S   OO   /   S   OH   /   S   AW   /   S   AH   /
S   AY   /   S   EE   /

7.   Once the S is established comfortably, continue practice for the sound using the words and phrases given below.

FORMING S – OTHER SUGGESTIONS

1.   Quite often it is possible to form a perfectly satisfactory Z, as in zoo. Practice for S can include comparing the two sounds in words:

seize/cease knees/niece norse/gnaws pass/parse
sown/zone sip/zip racer/razor sink/zinc seal/zeal
hiss/his fuss/fuzz loose/lose ice/eyes place/plays

2.   If the problem is a dental, or a TH substitute, paired
words comparing TH with S can be included:

thick/sick thank/sank thought/sought thin/sin
miss/myth pass/path worse/worth truce/truth
moss/moth force/fourth

Words to practise S

sit set sat sound sought soap save sand sell
serve sink

stop step staple stand stern start string
strong strength

decent assent assert assault missile missive
massive glasses

astir restrain estrange establish estimable
estimate esteem

disgust disgorge dismember disband dislocate
dyslexia

loose use close gas pass glass dress purchase
practice

Sentences to practise S

Several sick sailors asked for some sea salt.
The assassination of the assistant secretary surprised
several people.
The sisters sat snipping with scissors.
"Supper is served, Sir," said the servant in a sepulchral
voice.
The horse sustained several severe cuts.
Stay on the east side of the street.
Set the sack in the centre of the circle.
Six times six is thirty six.
The sun is stronger on the south side of the seat.
The snake stung swiftly and slid smartly away.

Clear and Dark L

There are two varieties of L commonly used in English. They are known technically as lateral sounds.

To form the clear L
The soft palate is raised to prevent the passage of air down the nose. The teeth are slightly apart. The tip of the tongue rises to contact and hold the gum ridge and the sides of the tongue are lowered, allowing the air to pass laterally over this position. Clear L has as a secondary articulation a raising of the front of the tongue towards the hard palate. It is this secondary articulation which forms the distinguishing quality between the two kinds of L.

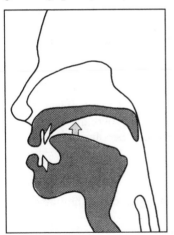 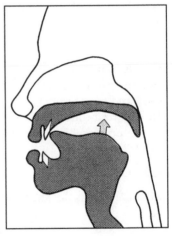

Formation of clear L (left) and dark L (right)

To form the dark L
The soft palate is raised to prevent the passage of air through the nose. The teeth are slightly apart. The tip of the tongue rises and contacts the gum ridge and the sides of the tongue are lowered, allowing the air to pass laterally over this position. The back of the tongue is raised

towards the soft palate (velum) during the formation of the sound, as a secondary articulation.

Occurrence of clear and dark L in English

Clear L is usually used before vowels and the 'y' sound, as in mill*i*on. Dark L is used at the ends of words, before consonants and sometimes as a whole syllable when it follows a consonant, for example: bottle settle kettle.

MAIN FAULTS

Distribution

There are many speakers who do not distinguish between the use of the two kinds of L and, as a result, may use one form or another exclusively. Since both sounds are identical, except for the secondary articulation, it is important to concentrate on the secondary aspects of the sound.

No use of L as a syllable

When dark L is final and preceded by T or D it usually has the value of a whole syllable. T or D should be exploded over the sides of the tongue, followed by the dark L and no intervening vowel. Words such as kettle and little, sound childish if a vowel is spoken between the T and the L.

Substitution of a vowel

In some speech, particularly Cockney, the tongue tip is not raised and held against the gum ridge. The result is a vowel with lip rounding. This only occurs when the L is final. For example reel becomes reoo, stale becomes staoo.

CORRECTION

1.   Having established the ability to make the two kinds of L, it is essential to establish the correct positions for them as they occur in common English.

2.   The *secondary* articulation is the vital element in establishing the difference. Remember that the front of the tongue rises for clear L and the back of the tongue for dark L.

3.   Word practice is necessary to establish the use of dark L as a syllable. It is important to retain the tongue against the gum ridge as the preceding consonant is said. If the tongue falls between the formation of the two sounds

a vowel will be heard. For example, when saying 'metal' the tongue should be held on the ridge during the formation of t; the sides of the tongue are then lowered and the T sound explodes over the sides of the tongue during the formation of L.

4.   Where a vowel is substituted at the end of a word, the raising of the tongue to the gum ridge should be practised slowly and deliberately.

EXERCISES

To establish clear L

1.   Raise the tongue tip to contact the gum ridge. Hold the tongue in this position and say a series of EE sounds.

2.   Hold the tongue tip on the gum ridge, say EE and allow the tongue tip to fall behind the lower teeth.

3.   Beating the tongue against the gum ridge say:

LEE   LEE   LEE   LEE   LEE   LEE

4.   Repeat the following words several times:

silly ceiling   silly ceiling   silly ceiling

5.   Repeat the following sequence:

OOLI   OHLI   AWLI   AHLI   AYLI   EELI

6.   Practise the words and sentences containing clear L.

To establish dark L

1.   Raise the tip of the tongue to contact and hold the gum ridge. Say a series of OO sounds.

2.   Hold the tongue tip on the gum ridge, say OO and allow the tongue tip to fall behind the lower teeth.

3.   Repeat OOL several times.

4.   Repeat the following sequence of sounds:

OOLG   OOLK / OOLG   OOLK / OOLG   OOLK

5.   Speak the following sequence:

OOLG   OHLG   AWLG   AHLG   AYLG   EELG
OOLK   OHLK   AWLK   AHLK   AYLK   EELK

6.   Use the practice words and sentences for dark L.

**To establish the sound at the ends of words such as
kettle and middle**

1.   Hold the tongue tip against the gum ridge and try
to say a T sound. Allow the T sound to explode over the
lowered *sides* of the tongue. Repeat this several times
without moving the tongue tip.

2.   Place the vowels in front of the sound achieved in
exercise 1. Note the rise of the tongue tip to the gum ridge
and hold it there while a T sound is attempted.

3.   Make the sound in exercise 1 but add an L sound.
Do not allow the tongue to fall between the T and the L.
Do this very slowly.

4.   Place the forefinger behind the upper front teeth,
raise the tongue tip to contact the gum ridge and feel the
underside of the tongue with the finger. Hold this position
and attempt to say T L *very* slowly.

5.   Retaining the finger behind the upper front teeth,
say the following sequence of sounds, feeling the underside of the tip of the tongue contact and hold the finger as
the TL sequence is said slowly:

BOOTL   BOHTL   BAWTL
BAHTL   BAYTL   BEETL

6.   Repeat exercise 5 without the use of the finger.

Words to practice clear L

leave   last   loiter   later   letter   lip   lap   lost
length   live   love   lend   loaned
alone   allow   silly   chilly   fellow   shallow   holy
hallow   hollow   believe
place   plastic   plank   blame   blue   blood   glue
glow   glare   slip   slide   slack

Words to practise dark L

killed   called   fold   silk   gold   sulk   hold   hailed
healed   mailed   mauled
almost   altogether   also   alter   falter   wealthy
healthy   cauldron
fill   feel   fool   mail   stale   steal   pull   full   grill
grail   careful   bashful

Sentences to practise clear L

The letter is likely to be lost.
He had long legs and leapt easily along the lane.
Millions of black and blue flies.
A little less, please.
The flames leapt into the loft.
It's foolish to leave a wallet lying around.
A lazy lion lurched along.
The lithe athlete leapt clear.
The pilot landed the plane smoothly.
The blood flowed slowly.

Sentences to practise dark L

Fill the pail full of coal.
He failed to sell the needles.
The ball of wool rolled away.
Filthy gold silk.
The wealthy fool stole the gold.
The milk yield fell all year.
Moles are making tunnels in the fields.
Harold fell and yelled for help.
The pool was full of tall reeds.
Hold the molten gold until it's almost cold.

Words to practise L as a syllable

settle kettle scuttle battle wattle fettle hurtle petal metal
cattle middle addle ladle cradle nodal meddle saddle
paddle handle

The TH Sound

There are two sounds represented by the letters TH in English. They have exactly the same formation except that one is spoken *without* voice, as in 'thick', and the other is said *with* voice, as in 'those'. They are known technically as dental fricatives.

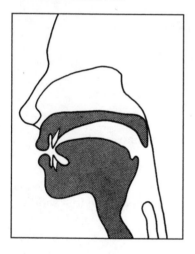

Formation of the TH sound

To form this sound
The soft palate is raised to prevent the passage of air through the nose. The tip of the tongue is held lightly against the upper front teeth, while the sides of the tongue hold the upper side teeth. Air is forced between the tongue tip and the teeth with audible friction. During the formation of TH, as in 'those', the voice is sounded. During the formation of TH, as 'thick', the voice is not sounded.

MAIN FAULTS

Substitution of F and V
In certain varieties of English, notably Cockney, F and V are directly substituted for TH.

Substitution of T and D

It is not uncommon to hear a direct substitution of T and D for TH.

CORRECTION

1. The placing of the tongue, lightly against the upper front teeth, is most important. The tongue should not be held tightly, causing an explosive sound when it is released.
2. It is not necessary to cause the tongue tip to protrude *beyond* the front teeth during the formation of this sound.

FORMING TH

1. Keep the teeth apart and hold the tip of the tongue *very* lightly against the upper front teeth. There should hardly be any sensation of contact between the tongue and the teeth. Blow several short sharp puffs of air over this position.
2. Take up the tongue position and try to say ER. A sound similar to TH, as in 'those', should be heard.
3. Speak the following sequence of sounds lifting the tongue slowly and carefully to make the TH sound:

> OOTHOO   OHTHOH   AWTHAW
> AHTHAH   AYTHAY   EETHEE

4. Keeping the tongue lightly against the upper teeth, alternate the voiced and unvoiced sounds several times.
5. Practise the two TH sounds followed by S and Z.
6. Practise the two TH sounds preceded by S and Z.
7. Speak the following combination of sounds, first with the unvoiced TH, then using the voiced TH:

> OOSTHS   OHSTHS   AWSTHS
> AHSTHS   AYSTHS   EESTHS

Words to practise unvoiced TH

> thick   thought   thong   thatch   thirty   theme
>   thumb   three   throng   thrift
> lethal   ethics   author   method   enthusiasm
>   cathedral   mathematics
> athletic   pathetic   breathless   filthy   sympathy
>   lengthy   pathos
> bath   worth   wreath   earth   wealth   broth   tenth
>   fifth   breath   mirth

Words to practise voiced TH

this that then their those though thus thither therefore

father mother heather weather further either gather northern heathen

bathe soothe clothe smooth loathe writhe with seethe

Sentences to practise unvoiced TH

Think of three themes.

The thieves took the path to the wealthy author's house.

The third, fourth and fifth breaths.

Three thousand three hundred and thirty three feathers.

Thank the pathetic youth for his sympathy.

The path leads through the thicket.

The mathematical thesis lacks method.

Think things out thoroughly.

Thursday is his seventh birthday.

Three free throws.

Sentences to practise voiced TH

Though they were there.

My father's other brother bathed frequently.

I loathe this smooth leather.

Gather the others together.

I'd rather not use leather either.

Smooth breathing is soothing.

Place the lathe there.

He breathes with several rhythms.

The heather blew hither and thither.

Whether the weather is hot.

The Glottal Stop

Description
This is a sound which occurs quite frequently in speech, often unnoticed, and which has no letter in ordinary spelling to represent it. The symbol used in the recording of speech to denote this sound is (?). In forming a glottal stop the vocal cords close together, and hold that position momentarily, preventing the passage of air into the mouth. When the vocal cords part and the air, which has compressed below the cords, is released, there is an unvoiced explosion. A cough may be regarded as a very exaggerated form of glottal stop.

MAIN FAULTS

Unlike the other individual sounds of speech described in this book, the problem with glottal stop is *not* learning how to develop a correctly articulated sound but, rather, learning to omit the sound where it is not required. There are many dialects of English which use glottal stop frequently, and as a substitute for other sounds.

Substitute for unvoiced plosive sounds
It is characteristic of certain forms of Cockney, Scottish, Lancashire and Yorkshire speech to substitute a glottal stop for the sounds P T K, particularly where these sounds occur between vowels, e.g. letter (le?er) people (peo?le) taking (ta?in).

Glottals before unvoiced plosives
Again in certain varieties of Southern, and some Eastern varieties of speech, a glottal stop may be inserted before P T and K in certain words. E.g. neu?tral, bu?ttress. The glottal stop is evident in the *silence* between the vowel and the consonant.

Glottal between vowels
Quite often a glottal is used between vowels to mark the boundaries of syllables; particularly where the second syllable is also stressed. E.g. co-operate (co?operate), creation (cre?ation), piano (pi?ano). This usually characterises a very careful kind of speech, often heard amongst public speakers and actors when they are being very emphatic. The incidence of glottal stops between vowels is not only confined to single words. It very often occurs between words where the final sound in the first word is a vowel and the word following begins with a vowel. E.g. better off (better?off), play away (play?away), dye it (dye?it).

Note: In the case of 'better off' the glottal may occur in an attempt to avoid a linking R sound and would be regarded as over-careful speech. There are numerous examples where this attempt to resist an R sound produces glottal stop. E.g. soda and water (sodarand water or soda?and water), law and order (lawrand order or law?and order), leisure activities (leisuractivities or leisure?activities).

The linking R is more commonly used where words end with U (the short neutral sound in oth*er*), AH or AW. It is indicated by spelling. E.g. other end (oth*er*end), car exhaust (carexhaust), more and more (moreand more).

Glottals before vowels in initial accented syllables
The glottal stop may occur, and quite often does, when the speaker gives particular emphasis to a word beginning with a vowel. Usually the first syllable of the word is an accented one. E.g. ?O, for a muse of fire. That's ?awful!, He's ?ignorant.

CORRECTION

1.	Concentration, in speaking, should be placed on the flow of the breath, rather than on the activity in the throat. This helps to relieve some of the unnecessary strain on the muscles of the throat.

2.	All exercises should be undertaken quietly, at first.

3.	In the case of glottal substituting for T or D, it is essential to establish the formation of those sounds first. Speaking slowly and breaking the words into separate syllables should assist this. For example, where the speaker would normally say 'bu?er' for 'butter', to practise this word as two very separate syllables, bu -tter, gradually increasing speed, is helpful.

4. Exercises for general breath control (see p. 20) and placing of the voice (see p. 40) assist in a fluent production of tone.

5. Exercises for relaxation, particularly of the throat and shoulders (see p. 12) form a necessary preliminary.

EXERCISES

1. Speak the following sequence of vowels, stressing the H sound when it occurs:

OO H OO   OH H OH   AW H AW
AH H AH   AY H AY   EE H EE

2. Repeat exercise 1 but form a very lightly sounded H.

3. Repeat exercise 2, but omit the H. Leave a silence where is should occur. During the silence imagine the breath continuing to pass over the tongue, before speaking the vowel a second time.

4. Speak each of the vowels, whispering them first, then gradually voicing them quietly. The passage from 'whispered' to 'spoken' should be continuous:

OH . . . . OO   OH . . . . OH
  Whisper-Speak   Whisper-Speak
AW . . . . AW
  Whisper-Speak
AH . . . . AH   AY . . . . AY
  Whisper-Speak   Whisper-Speak
EE . . . . EE
  Whisper-Speak

5. Speak the vowels, leaving a moment's silence between each. Imagine that the breath is passing over the tongue during that silence.

6. Speak the following words, preceding each with an H sound:

(H) uneven   (H) India   (H) after   (H) oozing
(H) alteration (H) apple   (H) awful
(H) elephant   (H) eating   (H) earnest

7. Speak the words again leaving a silence between each in which you imagine the breath passing over the

tongue. Concentrate on imagining the sound *in* the mouth and *not in the throat*.

8. Speak the following, placing an H between each of the words. Speak the second word strongly, with accent:

It's (H) uneven	His (H) apple	It's (H) awful
The (H) alteration	Stop (H) eating	In (H) earnest
An (H) elephant	You (H) after	It's (H) oozing
To (H) India		

9. Repeat exercise 8, leaving a silence between the words, during which you imagine that the H is said.

10. Repeat this, connecting the words, without a glottal on the accented first syllable of the second word.

EXERCISES FOR GLOTTAL SUBSTITUTIONS

1. Speak the following, ensuring that the consonants are formed:

OO   TOO / OH TOH / AW TAW /
AH   TAH / AY TAY / EE   TEE /

2. Speak the following, slowly, make the first vowel very long, noting the movement of the tongue towards the T sound:

OO ... TOO / OH ... TOH / AW ... TAW /
AH ... TAH / AY ... TAY / EE ... TEE /

3. Connect the sounds and increase the pace of delivery:

OOTOO   OHTOH   AWTAW
AHTAH   AYTAY   EETEE

Articulate the T sound very strongly.

4. Divide the following words into two very distinct syllables:

be-tter	ma-tter	beau-ty	pa-per
bu-tter	mu-tter	boun-ty	su-pper
bi-tter	mar-tyr	luck-y	su-per
ba-tter		jo-ker	wa-ter

Note carefully the sensation of raising the tongue to form the T sound, the raising of the back of the tongue for K sounds or the closing of the lips for P.

5. Repeat the words, closing the gap between the syllable, but retaining the movement of the tongue, or lips, for the consonant.

6. Speak the following, making the final consonant of the first word clearly and leaving a short silence before the second word:

cup of tea	but any	keep eating
sick of him	unlock it	get after
bet again	put over	take it

7. Speak the two words slowly, but continuously, noting the movement of either lips or tongue to form the final consonant of the first word.

8. Read the following passage, after noting where the glottal stop may intrude:

At the end of the episode, Arthur is seen to avoid an accident at Waterloo, involving an unknown object which arrives, unannounced, around a corner. 'Better and better,' mutters Arthur as he disappears into the Tube heading for Tottenham for a cup of tea.

Indistinct Speech

Speech is generally rendered indistinct or unintelligible when the consonants are omitted, substituted or incompletely articulated. The consonant sounds generally appear at the boundaries of syllables and words and help to shape the sound (the voice) into a recognizable pattern (speech). When those anticipated patterns are disturbed or incomplete the listener will have difficulty in understanding. It is important, therefore, to speak the consonants clearly and provide the appropriate and completed cues to the boundaries of a syllable and the word.

The reasons for such problems may be due to:

1. Lack of muscular effort, tone and dexterity.
2. Uncertainty about the subject.
3. Apprehension and nervousness in the speaking situation.

With regard to 2 and 3, some recommendations and exercises have ben given in the chapter entitled 'Relaxation' (p. 10). It is the purpose of this chapter to provide exercises which will deal with the technical aspects of Indistinct Speech, including more exercises to build the stength and dexterity of the lips, tongue and soft palate.

EXERCISES FOR THE LIPS

Pass the pens and pencils please.
Packing pickles poses problems.
Apparently the representative is appealing for support.
The apples appear to be dropping haphazardly.
The stupid spider disappeared into the upturned barrel.
The perspiring pianist performed perfectly.
Betty baked a better batch of buns.
Bobby burst the big blue balloon.

Please pack and post the parcel.
I bought a book about a boy who became a prince.
Why will you worry?
Wendy watched the weasel walking.
Where are the watches we wanted?
Wild winds and wet weather.
Walter watched while we were walking.
You are a fool to do it.
You lose too many shoes.
We choose the removing men.
The beautiful blue balloon.
Do go through and look at Sue.

EXERCISES FOR THE TONGUE

Leave the lazy lion alone.
If you delay longer we're likely to be late.
The dull light from the candle burned slowly in the lamp.
Lie on your pillow and swallow the pill.
The lorry was filled with bullion valued at three million
    lire.
Don't touch those taps till I return.
The butler stopped to eat a toffee.
I got wet while I was out.
Take a tube to Tewkesbury.
Let's eat a lot of tomatoes today.
He wrote his diary until dinner was ready.
He didn't want to admit that the leader was right.
It's terribly difficult to enunciate a lot of 't's'.
The door down the corridor slammed too.
Shall we shut the shop?
The shepherd had been shot in the shoulder.
Quick, catch and kick the ball.
The choir came carolling at Christmas.
He parked his car close to the cliff.
He grabbed the grapes greedily from grandad's garden.

EXERCISES FOR THE SOFT PALATE AND BACK
OF THE TONGUE

I'm thinking of singing a moving song.
Bring your gong along.
I think he got a drink from the tank.

In the spring the birds are singing and the donkeys braying.
I'm pulling a long length of string.
Rushing along fleeing from the angry Orang Outang.
Gather the grapes and crush them.
Going and getting Granny's gift.
A ragged beggar was swaggering with his dagger.
The car's gears crashed.
He was greedily grabbing the gravy.
More wagons making mud.
Can you be carrying the carrots from the garden?
Another car needs cleaning.
I'm making threatening noises.
He's getting the grey golf clubs.
Imagine mending the old thing.
I'm alone at home reading.
Playing a game of cards.
Speeding along the winding road.

CONSONANT EXERCISES

The following exercises pose words of more than one syllable with difficult combinations of consonants. Whisper them through, three times each. Speak them through slowly and accurately. Finally speak each sentence three times as quickly as accuracy will allow:

1. He made a number of accusations concerning his impecunious but meritorious companion.
2. There is a singular irregularity in using this word attributively.
3. Though contentious and obsequious his innocence was emphasised by his superficiality.
4. Energetic precautionary measures of unusual severity will be operated by general practitioners.
5. The professor of biological medicine's self-satisfaction aroused his audience to incomparable scepticism.
6. Arithmetical problems differ from those of differential calculus which deals with variable quantities.
7. Though published posthumously, *The Meticulous Horticulturist* earned unparalleled critical approval.
8. The traditional violation of professional conventions is undoubtedly intentional.

EXERCISES FOR WORD ENDINGS

Quite often the final consonants in a word are omitted and as a result the speaker's intended meaning is not clear. Many words depend on the final consonant for their distinction. For example the simple word bet can only be determined by hearing the final t. Otherwise it could be bed, ben, beck, bell and many others.

Speak the following, taking time to speak the final consonants (shown in bold) clearly. Pay particular attention to whether the consonant is voiced or unvoiced.Begin slowly on a whisper. Then introduce voice, gradually increasing the pace without losing the clarity and defininition of those final sounds.

1. In an act of magnificent courage the fireman leapt towards the burning shed.

2. The hard wood forest was ablaze with colours.

3. Get settled and start at the beginning.

4. The crowd was aghast at the last fast ball passed the post.

5. Settling down against the wall to shield himself from the wind the shepherd reached into his bag searching for his knife and the piece of wood which he was carrying. The clouds scudded across the sky darkening the light as the sheep bleated and huddled closely together. The sound of the bagpipes whining a plaintive dirge could be heard just beyond the church in the cleft of the valley below. All was sad, dark and bleak; it was not a good beginning to a night.

EXERCISES FOR GENERAL AGILITY OF THE ORGANS OF SPEECH

The following jingles and 'tongue-twisters' provide exercise for deft, clear and agile movements of the lips, tongue and soft palate. It is wise to follow the routine of whispering, then speaking them. Do not increase speed until you are absolutely sure you can master them at a moderate speed.

1.   My organs of articulation,
       Were a definite vexation,
       Until I said this silly rhyme
       Three times through.

2.   Many moaning men,
     Making music to the moon,
     Humming down their noses,
     It was a pleasant tune.

3.   Writing on a railway train
     Is very hard to do
     For it bumps you up and down
     And shakes you through and through.
     Clickety clack
     Down the track
     Heading for the station,
     I've put my pencil and paper away
     Till I reach my destination.

4.   Paul the ape provoked his keeper
     By ripping up banana skins.
     He dropped them in the baboon's cage
     Instead of specially provided bins.
     He pinched peanuts from the people
     Broke his box of plastic plates,
     He pushed big apples through the bars
     And banged and bashed his apey mates.

5.   Bright blue bubbles,
     Bobby blew and blew,
     Breathing, blowing, breathing,
     Behold . . .
     Bob became a bubble too!

6.   A weasel went walking by the water
     When a worm woke up and said,
     'Will you walk a little quieter,
     I was on my way to bed.'

7.   Two dukes tooting
     Two tunes on little flutes,
     'You knew "The Moon in June"
     When we played it on our lutes.'
     Duke One who tooted on the flute
     Was angry with Duke Two, who
     Although he knew 'The Moon in June'
     Could not keep his flute in tune
     So he played the lute, instead.

8.   Twenty tiny tap dancers
     Tapped to a bright light tune,
     Their routine was smart and dainty
     And they tapped and they did croon.
     Tip tap tappety tap tap tip
     Dippety, dippety tap tap dip.
     Teddy taught the tappers
     To tap and flick their feet,
     But it sometimes happened that the twenty
     Tried too hard, and missed a beat,
     So instead of
     Tip tap tappety tap tap tip
     Dippety, dippety, tap tap dip,
     It was
     Tip tappety tappety tip,
     Dippety tappety dip tip dip.

9.   A lazy lion lurched along
     A leafy country lane,
     Leaving lots of people
     With a tale too difficult to explain.

10. Big bottles of beer
     Buy and bring them here.

11. The clock ticks round
     With a monstrous sound
     We wait and wait
     But its very late
     And the dog cannot be found.

12. A little lady lives alone
     Close to a little lake
     She plants blue flowers
     To be watered with showers
     And clears leaves with her rake.

13. The teacher marked the book in red
     'Not very good' she crudely said
     'Your grammar's wrong,
     Your sentence too long,
     Why don't you use your head?'

14. The little kettle
    made of metal
    sang a subtle tune
    The little kettle
    made of metal
    merrily did croon.

15. Buy the big brown books
    Bound in bright board binders.

16. The singers sung it softly
    The singers sung it slow
    The singers sung it sadly
    The singers sung it low

    The band played it boldly
    The band played it long
    The band played it loudly
    The band played it strong

    The dancers danced it gently
    The dancers danced it fast
    The dancers danced it smoothly
    The dancers danced it last.

Note to Teachers

There are many approaches to the correction of speech faults, which the experienced and informed teacher will know. In this book I have tried to avoid, as far as possible, any controversial topic, confining myself to accepted fact and the presentation of exercises which I have personally found to be effective.

I am convinced that in order for the student to gain maximum benefit he or she should be presented with the information concerning his or her particular problem in as concise, methodical and accurate a way as possible.

There is no substitute for clear, progressive instruction, where the student is not inundated with a welter of relevant but insignificant detail. As you will know, it is often important to edit or rephrase what we know to be exact scientific description, in order to render it accessible and practical to a concerned student.

In attempting to make this a practical book, from which an untrained person might seek self-help, I have deliberately reduced the terminology. For example, no account of the Fortis/Lenis opposition in consonants is given, nor have I described the direction of the airstream as Egressive or Ingressive, believing that their inclusion will only complicate the description and, ultimately, have little significance in affecting the particular faults dealt with in this book. The learning and remembering of these terms only presents another challenge to the speaker; whereas his or her primary concern is to gain practical instruction, as easily as possible, in order that the correction can begin.

This principle is also demonstrated in the chapter on breathing, where I refer to the student placing his or her hand on the stomach in order to feel the diaphragm. I realise that it is anatomically impossible *actually* to feel the diaphragm. However, in expressing it this way I have found it to be a useful and ready instruction which gains the desired response.

In using this book, I would recommend that the description of the sounds and the diagrams are studied in some detail. This first stage is important to establish what is

required. The contrast between the inadequate formation and the desired one can be marked clearly at this early stage.

After clarifying exactly what is required, the exercises should be tackled slowly and methodically. They should never be rushed, ensuring that the goal for each is established before moving on. Results are unlikely at the very first attempt.

Encouragement is most important. The kind of teaching that depends on concentrated bullying is not likely to be permanently effective. Where possible, the attainment of the student should be stressed – even though it may be minimal compared with what has to be done.

I would suggest that correction should be undertaken in short bursts, with other, diverting material in a class of any length. To continue work for long sustained periods of time on just one problem stretches the concentration of the student well beyond anything productive. It may serve only to daunt and disappoint.

Finally, you will no doubt recognize the principles involved in each of the exercises and wish to add others of your own; this variation of approach can be very helpful. The following is a short, but selective, list of books which are recommended for further study or reference. A number of them contain an extension of the information presented in this book, and many of them make suggestions for other valuable exercises.

Phonetics
Gimson's Pronunciation of English, revised by Alan Cruttenden
    (Edward Arnold)
Phonetics, J. D. O'Connor (Pelican)
In each there is a full discussion of the formation of sounds in Received Pronunciation, as well as an account of many regional and foreign variations.

Disorders of voice and speech
Voice and Articulation, Van Riper and Irwin (Pitman
    Medical)
The Voice and its Disorders, Margaret C. L. Greene (Pitman
    Medical)
Improving the Child's Speech, Virgil Anderson (Oxford
    University Press, New York)
These are specialist books aimed at the speech therapist.

They give a clear insight into the many complexities of voice and speech disorders. They are not recommended in order to extend the scope of the speech teacher's work, but to serve as an indication and a warning as to which faults are more properly referred to a speech therapist or for qualified medical help.

General voice and speech training
Training the Speaking Voice, Virgil Anderson (Oxford University Press, New York)
Voice and Speech in the Theatre, J. Clifford Turner (A & C Black)
These two books offer a comprehensive account of the processes of voice and speech, together with many exercises for improvement.